BUSES IN THE MIDLANDS 1990s AND 2000s

MATT COOPER

AMBERLEY

First published 2025

Amberley Publishing
The Hill, Stroud
Gloucestershire, GL5 4EP

www.amberley-books.com

ISBN 978 1 3981 2264 2 (print)
ISBN 978 1 3981 2265 9 (ebook)

British Library Cataloguing in Publication Data.
A catalogue record for this book is available from the British Library.

Typesetting by SJmagic DESIGN SERVICES, India.
Printed in the UK.

EU GPSR Authorised Representative
Appointed EU Representative: Easy Access System Europe Oü, 16879218
Address: Mustamäe tee 50, 10621, Tallinn, Estonia
Contact Details: gpsr.requests@easproject.com, +358 40 500 3575

Introduction

For the majority of the twentieth century the buses and coaches of Midland Red dominated the transport scene across central England. In a similar vein to London Transport this large organisation designed and built vehicles to their own specification with Carlyle works, by comparison, similar to 'Aldenham'. Staff took great pride in working for 'the red' and before presenting themselves to the public would use full-length mirrors displayed at depots which detailed what to check regarding their personal appearance. Our journey through the Midlands is based on the original operating area of this organisation, the East and West Midlands. Midland Red was eventually split into four operating units, each of which still exist today, albeit none of them have vehicles painted red.

During the period some operator's names changed several times, usually when under new ownership. For ease, abbreviations have been applied: Midland Red North (MRN) Midland Red South (MRS) Midland Red West (MRW) Nottingham City Transport (NCT) and Travel West Midlands (TWM).

In the post-deregulation era, there were considerable changes occurring to the routes or networks previously operated by the state-owned National Bus Company (NBC). Many newcomers entered the ring to try their hand at bus operation, bringing with them all sorts of vehicles, which were decorated in a range of liveries. A number of municipally owned companies operated within the region, who also adapted themselves to the new operating environment. Most would eventually be sold to the larger groups which were developing throughout this period, with consolidation also occurring among many of the former NBC companies. The Perth-based Stagecoach Group would achieve a worldwide portfolio whilst others, such as the Wellglade Group, would remain focused on a more specific geographical area and only making acquisitions close to it.

European influences to vehicle types began around the time of privatisation, which would replace the models inherited from NBC. As a result, smaller operators would make good use of these second-hand vehicles, which would also provide considerable interest for the enthusiast. However, in a few cases, vehicle presentation wasn't always at the forefront of some operator's priorities, leading to a questionable image of modern public transport. Would Mr and Mrs Bloggs leave their locally built Rover at home and try the bus? This was the era where passengers became customers and considerable emphasis was placed on customer experience.

Trent, considered market leaders in many respects, was at the forefront of this subject, launching Rainbow Routes in the early 1990s. The philosophy of such routes was simple; staff were trained to a high standard offering a range of straightforward ticketing options aboard a very modern fleet of buses. From an early stage the products from Optare were chosen, with the smart designs of the bodybuilder complementing Trent's desire to improve the image of bus travel. A pleasing example that showed the more positive effects of privatisation and moved away from the more common 'cut-throat competition' approach where, between 6 a.m. and 6 p.m., everyone chased the same group of passengers.

In the years preceding privatisation NBC introduced significant numbers of minibuses, a type that would play an important role in the late 1980s/early 1990s. Carlyle works in Birmingham, historically associated with Midland Red, became a major hub for minibus conversion and bodybuilding. Many of the earlier styles would evolve into comfortable and stylish models or towards larger 'midibus' types. For the operator these vehicles were a useful tool in developing new networks or expanding existing operations, making them more cost effective. Across the Midlands there was post-deregulation 'chess' played, with strategic moves being made by those setting up new routes or networks, trading with those they sought to compete against.

Birmingham was no stranger to bus manufacturing, with MCW producing vehicles at its Washwood Heath premises. In 1977 MCW launched the Metrobus, a stylish product bearing close resemblance to earlier models produced when in partnership with Swedish manufacturer Scania. With a policy of buying local vehicles it was inevitable West Midlands Travel would operate the MCW Metrobus, and between 1978 and 1989 over 1,100 were received, forming the backbone of the double-deck fleet. Scania would launch its own range of products from 1980, which would also prove popular with operators across the region.

The Leyland Lynx was another vehicle associated with the West Midlands. Being launched at a time of great uncertainty made it a very different marketplace to that of its predecessor, the National. Sales were not as significant as hoped, with just over a thousand units produced between 1986 and 1992. West Midlands Travel would be the largest user with 256 examples, local neighbour Midland Red West taking fifty.

During the mid-1990s there was a large-scale introduction of low-floor vehicles to the UK with a subsequent shift towards this accessible type of vehicle. By the end of the decade most manufacturers' final new step-entrance vehicles had rolled off the production line. Nottingham's unique body styling had by this stage given way to more standard types, although a batch of 'bendy-buses' were launched around the turn of the new millennium. The company hoped their finer points would be seen by council planners who may have preferred them to light rail. This wasn't the case and Nottingham Express Transit (NET) opened in March 2004. It seems the UK does not share the same support or passion as its European counterparts for this type of articulated transport, with a total of just over 800 used in the UK between 1979 and 2007. Birmingham, Coventry and Leicester would also give them a go, all of which were eventually replaced by tried-and-tested double-deck designs.

The Midlands Metro light rail services began operating from Wolverhampton in May 1999, with its iron roads gradually reaching the heart of Birmingham and destinations southwards in the years that followed. This impacted the local buses with operators revising their routes accordingly to serve the repositioned on-street bus stops which were pushed further towards the periphery of the city centre. By contrast, passengers at Leicester and Nottingham have the use of two bus stations each per city!

Ownership of companies large and small would change throughout the 1990s and 2000s. Several municipal companies would be privatised, West Midlands Travel being the largest. As with a number of other operators it was initially sold to a management buyout but later acquired by one of the 'big groups' soon afterwards, National Express Group. Grampian Regional Transport (GRT) purchased Leicester Citybus from the council in 1994 following a similar purchase at Northampton the previous year. Both were united by shared management, engineering functions and a joint livery. GRT kept a 'local' family feel with a greater degree of autonomy, which would be lost in later years under First Group control. This latter period was also characterised by numerous unfamiliar bus types and liveries. The cyclical nature of driver shortages and recruitment would often see groups ferried up and down the M1 to the depot in greatest need. This led Leicester drivers to work mid-engined vehicles and Northampton drivers having to get used to the marble-run type change dispensers.

Several of the UK's major routes criss-cross the region presenting opportunities for coach operators to utilise on a regular basis or to simply pass through. The established paths of National Express have now been joined by newcomers such as Megabus offering the passenger a greater choice of travel options.

Manufacturing and distribution remain major industries in the Midlands today with the products and services they provide as varied as the bus services you will find on offer. Operations of a very rural nature exist together with high-frequency services to be found in the region's cities. As we travel through the Midlands I hope memories of this period will be evoked and the images recorded used as a background to the scene to be found today.

My sincere thanks are due for the photographic assistance of Raymond Bedford, Malcolm Crowe, Jeff Jones and Kevin Lane. There are some other unattributed shots which I've chosen from my collection. I am grateful to Alison Flowers and the staff at Amberley Publishing for taking the project on and to Bob Jackson for advice and assistance. Lastly, a special mention to my wife and family for their understanding, help, support and patience throughout this book's creation, frequently losing me for many hours at a time!

Throughout the book's compilation I often found myself thinking I wish I had taken more pictures, perhaps not always appreciating that today's scene is tomorrow's historical viewpoint. Our journey across the region is interspersed with several themed groups which I hope will be enjoyed.

With no official soundtrack to accompany this book you are invited to use the wonders of online video-sharing platforms to help fully immerse yourself in the era, especially with some sharing the wonderful sounds of the vehicles used during that period. Or perhaps more appropriately play your favourite group or artist of the time through the media of CDs, LPs or tapes!

Our journey begins at St Margaret's bus station in Leicester where First Wessex Transbus Plaxton Paragon-bodied Volvo B12M 6309 (later 20524) (WX52 HSX) calls on 8 May 2008 while working the mammoth 330 service. One journey per day ran the full length of the route from Nottingham to Penzance, with a total journey time of twelve and a half hours!

In 1996 Derby City Transport received five new East Lancs-bodied Scania L113s delivered in their yellow-based 'City Rider' livery. 3493 (N433 XRC) was caught unloading at Gravel Street in Leicester on 8 May 2008 when all five, plus two others, were based at Coalville. Numbered DO33 when new, the number 2193 had also been carried. Routes 152 and 153 were hourly, the latter originating from Market Bosworth.

Should your visit to St Margaret's bus station have been that enjoyable a postcard was available as a souvenir. The modern facility opened on 3 May 1985 and has been the subject of two subsequent refurbishments. This early 1990s view details period vehicle types and liveries along with Midland Fox's Sandacre depot, centre-left with a small flagpole. By 1992 this was home to just over 100 minibuses (or Fox Cubs) but was later closed, its new purpose being a nightclub. (Author's collection)

Services operated by Leicester Citybus (later First Group) utilised Haymarket bus station, located at the top of a 'wedge' between the main thoroughfares of Charles Street and Haymarket. On 28 April 2008 First's Alexander ALX400-bodied Volvo B7TL 32098 (new as 235) (KP51 WDD) departs with a very light load.

A batch of seventy-five Leyland Nationals were delivered to Midland Red in early 1977, coded N6, as represented by 605 (NOE 605R), which operated among 'south' division depots throughout its life. Under Western Travel ownership thirty-one of the type were upgraded as 'National Mark 3s', receiving DAF engines and internal refurbishment. At St Margaret's bus station on 18 January 1994 upgraded 605 was laying over after making the two hour and twenty minute journey from Coventry via Nuneaton. The vehicle would remain in service until October 2003. (Jeff Jones)

A quicker link between Coventry and Leicester was offered by Arriva Midlands route X6, taking one hour and ten minutes end-to-end. At Pool Meadow on 8 May 2008 East Lancs European-bodied Scania 2175 (N175 PUT) wore the 'inter-urban'-style livery, which would later become Arriva's standard application. The generic 'City Linx' legend was applied to a number of Arriva Midlands services.

Stagecoach Warwickshire's Prime Line 48 was the combination of a number of existing routes which, when viewed on a map, formed a 'Y' shape, Coventry being at the base Nuneaton in the middle diverging to either Atherstone or Leicester. Group standard branding featured on Plaxton Pointer 2-bodied Dennis Dart SLF 34113, which was new to Stagecoach East London's Stratford depot numbered SLD113. On 8 May 2008 it was passing Coventry City Hall en route for Leicester, with three journeys per hour taking this path.

A batch of similar vehicles, received new, ran alongside the former London Darts and were badged Transbus Pointer-bodied Transbus Dart. Last of the batch of nine, 34499 (KX53 VNL) was loading mid-stand at Nuneaton bus station on 8 May 2008 in a manner which could frequently be seen.

In 2008 routes 55, 56 and 57 between Nuneaton and Coventry via Bedworth were rebranded as 'Matrix' with fourteen newly delivered Alexander Enviro 200-bodied MAN 14.240 to operate them. Part of a larger batch shared with Northampton depot, the route branding was to a more local style as depicted by first of the batch, 39680 (KX08 KZO), recorded in Trinity Street, Coventry, 10 June 2008.

First Leicester received a batch of Wright Eclipse-bodied Volvo B7Ls in April 2002, their fleet numbers following on from the Optare Excels. 313 (KV02 VVY) had been delivered with a '51' plate but was re-registered before entering service. Laying over at Charles Street on 20 April 2003, the bus would later be numbered 66320. With its rather awkward internal layout the B7L didn't sell in great numbers, with First Group being the only major user of the type.

Sprucing up the double-deck fleet from mid-December 2000 were twelve Volvo B7TLs carrying Alexander ALX400 bodywork. Thirty-five more followed in January 2002 including 233 (KP51 WCN) and 250 (KP51 WBU), which are resting at Abbey Park Road depot on Sunday 20 April 2003. Later renumbered 32092 and 32084 respectively, the destination of the former shows it worked one of the Saturday night bus routes. They are accompanied by the last of the Volvo B7L batch 325 (KV02 VVM).

In early 2005 twenty-one further Volvo B7TLs were received, this time carrying Wright Eclipse Gemini bodywork. Nicknamed 'Nokia buses' as the layout of the front-end glass resembled the shape of the popular mobile phone, Group national numbers were applied from new. 32632 (KP54 KBJ), caught at Charles Street, Leicester, on 28 April 2008, was one of four initially used at Northampton. In keeping with the name of the pub, standard First Group policy at that time dictated no local identifiers be used, with the Overground brand also discontinued.

During the Midland Fox era considerable variety featured in the double-deck fleet, a theme which continued under Arriva ownership. Twenty-eight Northern Counties Palatine-bodied Volvo Olympians were received in 1998, with 4621 (R621 MNU) being one of four based at Coalville. Captured in Leicester city centre on 28 April 2008, it shows Arriva too were not fans of 'localism'.

Confidence Bus & Coach built up a fleet of seventy vehicles housed over two depot sites. Wearing the battleship-inspired livery, ECW-bodied Leyland Olympian XWY 476X was recorded in the city centre on 28 April 2008. New to West Riding in 1982, the bus passed through several subsequent owners, including Isle of Man Transport (registered DMN 82H), before acquisition in July 2001. It entered preservation in August 2018.

Midland Fox double-decker variety as evidenced in this city centre view, with the main feature being Wigston-based 4524 (G524 WJF), one of five Alexander RL-bodied Leyland Olympians new in January 1989. Under Arriva ownership the batch moved to Merseyside where they joined examples of similar appearance. The Bristol VR was acquired from South Midland and an ex-London Transport 'DMS' can just be seen. Midland Fox would operate numerous examples of this type, which was banished from London after a very short lifespan, which was echoed by bendy-buses in more recent times. (Author's collection)

Arriva Midlands 4012 (FJ56 OBL) was one of fourteen Wright Eclipse Gemini-bodied Volvo B7TLs based at Southgates. More commonly found in the fleet were 'Pulsar Gemini' vehicles of a similar appearance and the model name applied by Wright to DAF/VDL 250 chassis. Carrying generic 'Local Linx' branding, specific route and fare details are discreetly displayed around the vehicle.

New as First Leicester 227, Alexander ALX400-bodied Volvo B7TL 32070 (KP51 VZW) was recorded at Humberstone Gate on 28 April 2008. Later transferred to Bristol for university services, it would also work for First Kernow.

Proudly serving Leicester from their base at Glenfield was Hylton & Dawson, who had a liking for the Bedford marque. This is exemplified on CAX 14V, a YNT type with Duple Dominant II body seen in Haymarket on 18 January 1994. New to BEBB Llantwit Fardre, it was acquired from Bailey of Kirkby-in-Ashfield in 1988 and later re-registered HDZ 626. Their principal service was the 94 competing with First, who became the sole operator from mid-2005 after H&D closed. Mr Kiesa's Discotheque is now also a distant memory but has a popular fan club online. (Jeff Jones)

Leicester Citybus were pioneers of the Dennis Dominator, which was introduced in 1977, deliveries continuing until 1989, most with the combination of Gardner engine and Voith gearbox. New in late 1984 were a trio carrying East Lancs bodywork with an Alexander-inspired look. This was a specification chosen by Sheffield Mainline, who had exchanged the brand-new double-deckers for three of Leicester's Dennis Dorchester coaches. 84 heads through a quiet city centre wearing the pre-GRT maroon and cream livery. Interestingly, under First Group ownership, the buses transferred to Mainline. (Author's collection)

Northampton Transport acquired a significant number of school contracts from April 1996, for which vehicles from fellow GRT-owned companies were acquired. Leicester's East Lancs-bodied Dennis Dominators 180 and 183 were renumbered 201 and 202 at NT, with the latter captured here at Drapery on 6 August 1997 wearing the Leicester/Northampton GRT-inspired livery and full local fleet name.

In February 2002 nineteen Dennis Dominators were allocated to Leicester with ten at Northampton. At Abbey Park Road depot on 20 April 2003 were a group from the batch registered E-HNR with East Lancs bodywork. 94 and 92 were painted the last standard Leicester and Northampton scheme introduced by First Bus, while 91 and 89 behind them wear the experimental white, green and yellow livery applied around this time. It would be fair to say whichever depot they worked from the sound from these vehicles certainly dominated the local environment!

With private hire work in mind, Alexander RV-bodied Volvo Citybus 87 (F87 DVV) was transferred from Northampton to Leicester in April 1997 and renumbered 282. It retained coach seats on both decks, was fitted with a tachograph and given 'dateless' identity LSU 717, previously used on a Leyland Leopard. It would also work local services as captured in this view on 'yellow line 54'. Returning to Northampton on 19 May 2000, its condition was superior to its stablemates, which had been subjected to a depot flood in 1998 and vandal attack in 1999. (Author's collection)

Anstey Buslines (renamed Centrebus in 2001) operated an assortment of double-deckers of varying origin on a network of city routes, which competed against Arriva and First. The specification of this Alexander RV-bodied Volvo Citybus indicates it was new to Tayside and also worked for their successor Travel Dundee. On 28 April 2008 G101 PES provides competition on the Beaumont Leys corridor.

Twelve Volvo Olympians with Alexander bodywork were transferred from Glasgow to Leicester in July 2000. All livery variations were carried by the batch, numbered 180 to 191, which by February 2002 were already being transferred to other First companies. In as acquired condition 188 (P188 TGD) was loaned to Northampton and on 18 August 2000 caught at The Racecourse operating a P&R service for the annual balloon festival. Later numbered 34288 in First's national series between March 2002 and April 2014, the bus worked within the Group at Essex, Worcester and Stoke-on-Trent.

MRW operated very few double-deck vehicles and the only examples received new were five Transbus ALX400-bodied Transbus Tridents for Redditch. Last of the batch 33405 (VX54 MVB) was recorded at Winyates Centre on 17 June 2008 working circular route 57 (anti-clockwise). Together with the 58, these high-frequency services utilised many bus lanes around the estates, which were often referred to as 'tracks'.

In 2003 Volvo replaced the B7L with the B7RLE, allowing for a more logical interior to be applied by bodybuilders. First Group continued to favour products offered by Wright, the Eclipse Urban style fitted to twenty-six examples received by the Midlands division in 2005. Northampton initially received ten of this batch, which after only twelve months' service transferred to Leicester or Worcester. One such vehicle was 66968 (KX05 MJO), seen in Leicester on 28 April 2008 with minimal branding. The bus would later become one of 'Doncaster's Smart Buses'.

Under GRT Group ownership some interesting and more unusual marques appeared in their constituent fleets. This continued during the early years of First Bus ownership, with Leicester receiving a batch of ten integrally built Optare Excels. Numbered 301 to 310, they were registered on 1 August 1997 allowing for the new annual prefix letter to be applied to their select series marks. Delivered in a cream and red livery, standard First Group 'low-floor' livery soon followed as detailed on 309 when viewed at Abbey Park Road depot. In February 2002 the bus became 60158 when it transferred to Manchester with the rest of the batch under a policy of grouping vehicles of similar type together. (Author's collection)

'Variety is the spice of life' was perhaps the unofficial motto of First Leicester and Northampton in terms of vehicles and liveries. A pair of Volvo B6s acquired from First Capital forms the left-hand row. A green roof and skirt featured on the Northern Counties Paladin body of 432 (L5 GML), with 436 (L674 RMD) behind displaying Alexander Dash bodywork. Assisting vehicle availability was Alexander ALX200-bodied Volvo B6BLE R630 GSC on loan from Volvo and numbered 004 for its stay. Of similar appearance was V424 GGD but with ALX300 body and B10BLE chassis. ECW-bodied Leyland Olympian C720 NNN belonged to Kinch Bus and formed part of the outstation allocation on 20 April 2003.

On the same date, can you spot the odd pair out? Dominating the scene in a variety of liveries are East Lancs-bodied Dennis Falcons from the batch 611 to 619 registered in the series H-EJF. Sitting in the middle 621 (K621 SBC) with similar chassis carries bodywork by Northern Counties. Northampton's Duple 300-bodied Volvo B10M 112 (G112 ENV) was on loan.

More single-deck variety was introduced to Leicester from 2003 with several Leyland Lynxes transferred from First Wyvern (MRW). 1136 and 1137 were from a batch of fifty new in 1990 and were on loan at Northampton depot between 5 July and 8 August 2003. On 16 July the pair were bookended by Aberdeen Leyland Atlanteans at St James depot. The Centro sticker displayed in the windscreen of 1136 confused some intending passengers!

By the time the Leicester, Northampton and Wyvern fleets were renumbered into First's national series a more logical pattern had been adopted. Fourteen Lynxes were in use at Leicester by the time of this 28 April 2008 view of 62713 (G113 HNP) at Charles Street. The original side panels had been replaced and a 'willow leaf' applied, which was originally intended to denote a low-floor vehicle.

Vehicles from the fleet of Wolverhampton-based Travel Express ran in their previous owner's colours, Black Prince of Morley in this case, and were also fitted with fareboxes. D603 ACW was the fifty-second production Lynx and had a very varied career. New in April 1987, it was initially used by Leyland as a demonstrator before joining Jubilee Coaches in Stevenage and later Luton & District. On 13 August 2004 it was heading along Stevenson Street beside New Street station. Today the bright, airy, futuristic design of 'Grand Central' occupies the space above the station and only trams can now be caught from this thoroughfare. (Author's collection)

Following a series of trials in 1986 WMPTE chose the Leyland Lynx as its standard single-deck vehicle, eventually building up a fleet totalling 256. All achieved long careers around the West Midlands, with most sold on for further service. A gloomy 23 April 1999 saw 1272 loading in Edgbaston Street on route 15S, which ran off-peak to a ten-minute frequency.

Nottingham City Transport was also a keen supporter of the Lynx, with twenty-five received in 1988/9. The clean lines of the bodywork were complimented by the smart livery on 741 as it rested between trips at Trinity Square on 19 April 1994. Bus Eireann would later operate the vehicle, principally on school duties, numbered LS17 and registered 89 D 52274. Fish and chips can still be purchased from Moulin Rouge! (Jeff Jones)

A contemporary vehicle to the Lynx was launched by Optare in 1988. The Delta was offered exclusively on the DAF SB220 chassis and as with all the Leeds-based bodybuilder's products styling was eye-catching, a positive step towards improving the image of bus travel and attracting custom. This would complement Trent's 'Rainbow routes' concept and 314 was caught in Derby on 26 July 1995. (Jeff Jones)

A combination favoured by the Stagecoach Group between 1992 and 1998 was Alexander's Singapore-styled P-type bodywork coupled to the ever-reliable Volvo B10M chassis. The final seven for MRS entered service in February 1998 alongside similarly registered low-floor vehicles. Nuneaton was the home of 20221 where at that town's bus station on 8 May 2008 it was recorded working a 'Matrix' route. At the time automatic air fresheners were fitted to this and other Warwickshire-based vehicles – with passengers encouraged to inform the company of their preferred scent.

Volvo's low-floor B10BLE with Alexander ALX300 bodywork, one of twelve such examples in the Arriva Midlands fleet, was loading at the same location on the same date. Half of the batch was based at Hinkley, which the 158 served en route to Leicester, with Arriva retaining the more traditional route number. Operations in Hinkley would pass to Centrebus in September 2013.

Several Alexander PS-bodied Volvo B10Ms were transferred to United Counties during the mid-2000s with 20218 (P218 HBD) arriving from MRS already carrying a Northampton registration mark. The type was well suited to the X7 and the bus was caught departing St Margaret's bus station for its home town on 8 May 2008. The 'Limited stop' sign in the windscreen applied to stops in the Leicester and Northampton boroughs.

Route X7 was previously numbered X60/X61 and jointly operated with Midland Fox, an arrangement which lasted until 1998. East Lancs European-bodied Scania 33 (N433 XRC) was the last of a batch of five new to fellow company Derby, whose livery and fleet number sequence it still carried when viewed at Northampton's Greyfriars bus station on 1 September 1997.

Arriva would continue to provide a service between Market Harborough and Leicester numbered X3. Interesting vehicles were still feature on the route as exemplified by 4698 (49 XBF, L94 HRF), one of a pair of Optare Spectra-bodied DAF DB250s new to Stevensons in 1993 departing St Margaret's bus station on 28 April 2008. The duo were utilised across a number of Midlands depots.

At the busy transport hub of Market Harborough Square on 10 June 2008 Woods Coaches Alexander ALX200-bodied Dennis Dart (HJZ 9928, W871 VGT) was loading for Foxton, famed for its canal lock flight. Acquired from Epsom Buses, the twenty-eight seater would soon become 504 with Centrebus before one final move to Arriva Midlands for use in Hinkley.

Leicestershire County Council supported a useful link between Leicester and Peterborough, largely following the A47, which had been numbered X47 and 747 over the years. Midland Fox's minibuses were branded 'Fox Cub' with M337, a Dormobile Routemaker-bodied Mercedes-Benz 709D, joining the set from Stevensons, the source of a number of similar vehicles. Peterborough's Queensgate bus station was the location on 8 September 1995. (Jeff Jones)

Oakham is the largest town within Rutland served by a route from Peterborough via Stamford. Kimes of Folkingham received Wright Cadet-bodied FX04 TJY in May 2004, which was branded for the service and carried the fleet numbers R4 and S4 during its career. The former number was displayed when seen at Peterborough on 5 April 2008. The service would pass to Centrebus, as would the vehicle, which was later re-registered PJZ 9450.

Bellamy's Coaches of Nottingham offered an interesting service between Nottingham and Mablethorpe. Numbered 200, an assortment of coaches was used on the epic four-hour journey. Awaiting custom at Lincoln bus station while heading east on 22 March 2008 was S45 KSM, a fifty-five-seat Plaxton Premiere-bodied Volvo B7R new to Mc Ewan of Amisfield in October 1998 and acquired in March 2003.

National Express service 210 linked Wolverhampton to London Gatwick with nine journeys operating each way. One of the intermediate calling points was Banbury bus station where West Drayton-based Irizar Century-bodied Scania NXL15 (YN05 WJA) was about to call on 8 March 2010. These coaches, which featured leather seating, were used to upgrade National Express services from 2004 and the livery variation was showing support for Birmingham's Irish community.

Reversing off the stand at the old Bridge Street bus station in Banbury was MRS 871 (F871 UAC), a Robin Hood-bodied Iveco Daily 49.10 based at Leamington Spa, one of a pair new in 1989. Like Mercedes-Benz, Iveco had great success in the UK with minibus chassis but their single- and double-deck products were not as successful. (Author's collection)

A new fox on the block from 1997 was Banbury-based Claydon Fox. A smart fleet of mini coaches was operated in overall white as exemplified by YN11 AYO, a Plaxton Cheetah-bodied Mercedes-Benz Vario 0816D. On 25 February 2015 it was captured departing Flore C of E Primary School for Warwick Castle where their reception class were heading for the day.

At the time Stagecoach Holdings purchased the Western Travel Group in December 1993 thirty-two vehicles were allocated to Banbury depot including a small number of coaches. New as BVP 788V, Plaxton Supreme IV Express-bodied Leyland Leopard, fleet number 6, received a Leyland TL11 engine in March 1985 and had spent the majority of its career at Rugby. Cherished registration 3273 AC had been replaced with RNV 445V by the time of this 14 July 1997 view in Banbury depot, indicating its withdrawal was imminent.

Viewed at the same location on 26 November 2009, Alexander ALX200-bodied Volvo B6BLE 31365 (P365 DSA) was one of six such vehicles allocated to the depot. The relatively simplistic nature of service 500 can be appreciated by the map displayed in the first nearside window with the route number originating with Midland Red. The bus had been transferred from Glasgow and would return to Scotland for a subsequent life with McColl's of Dumbarton. (Raymond Bedford)

Four ECW-bodied Leyland Olympians were allocated to Nuneaton depot in September 1989 when this view at Showbus, Woburn Abbey, was recorded with the bus and its crew immaculately turned out. Later receiving Stagecoach Group national number 14932, it would operate from several other MRS depots, and attend several other Showbus events, before withdrawal in October 2006. This was the same year four ADL Tridents (18502–5) had been delivered to Nuneaton but soon swapped with Stagecoach South (Andover) for ADL Darts (34641–4). (Author's collection)

The first new double-deckers for MRS since 1985 were received in February 1999 consisting of seven Alexander RL-bodied Volvo Olympians for Leamington Spa depot. With Coventry DVLA office closed Northampton registrations were issued as shown on 16615 (S915 ANH), new as 915. An LED blind had recently been fitted when seen loading at Upper Parade on 8 March 2010 on one of the busy routes which catered for students of Warwick and Coventry universities.

Seven Alexander RL-bodied Leyland Olympians of 1988 vintage were transferred to Rugby depot from United Counties for use on school contracts. They would, at times, also stray onto local services as depicted by 14026 (F626 MSL) working through the town centre en route to Clifton-upon-Dunsmore on 8 May 2008.

The busy corridor between Sydenham and Coventry was revamped in 2005 to feature a distinctive colour scheme and routes prefixed with a 'U'. Members from the Alexander RL-bodied batch of Volvo Olympians had the scheme applied, eight of which were together in this 11 July 2010 view whilst working P&R duties for Silverstone F1 event. The livery would change again in 2011 to a more corporate style with red as the majority colour.

The depot at Station Approach in Leamington Spa was opened in mid-1990 and, as signage on the main building suggests, housed vehicles from MRS and G&G Travel. There is much variety in terms of vehicles and liveries in this view, giving a real flavour of the allocation at the time. Alexander Dash-bodied Volvo B6 456 was about to head out for another day's work on 18 November 1994. Its time at Leamington was brief, moving to Banbury then Cambridge, where it was initially numbered 308 and later 30556. It remained around Cambridge after April 2004 when sold to Go Whippet. The depot closed in 2017, its close proximity to the railway station appealing to developers, with the area now occupied by numerous apartments. (Jeff Jones)

Alexander's ALX range of low-floor products succeeded models such as the Dash, with the ALX200 being the midibus offering. Stagecoach Group ran examples on Volvo B6RLE and Dennis Dart SLF chassis, the class code 33, as depicted, applied to the latter type. From a batch of eleven new to Swindon 33911 was one of a pair transferred to Leamington featuring appropriate suffix letters and new LED destination blind. The bus loads on Upper Parade on 8 March 2010.

M. J. De Courcey was a significant force in the Coventry area since 1972, operating from a base at Baginton. Despite its Exeter registration, N453 VOD, the vehicle spent the majority of its life as Stagecoach Ribble 642, later passing to Blazefield Holdings. The Alexander Sprint-bodied Mercedes-Benz 709D was one of four acquired from Lancashire United in 2002, initially carrying De Courcey's Rural Rider branding. It was captured laying over at Pool Meadow bus station in Coventry on 8 May 2008.

Wright of Ballymena produced the smart Nimbus model with MRS operating twenty-four of the type coupled to the longer Mercedes-Benz 811D chassis. Six were named after former local collieries, as depicted on 416, with eight DP-seat examples given the names of animals. This July 1992 view predates Pool Meadow's refurbishment. (Author's collection)

The 'Primelines' brand featured on a number of routes operated by several operators across the West Midlands area. A jazzy colour scheme had originally featured, which Stagecoach later replaced with a more standard style as can be seen. Nuneaton depot received thirteen ADL Pointer 2-bodied ADL Darts principally for route 48. However, on New Year's Day 2010 34496 was viewed at Banner Lane terminus, Tile Hill, working one of a number of special services that day.

With Primelines' strapline featuring as part of its route branding Travel Coventry 4688 (BU05 HFE) passes Pool Meadow bus station whilst crossing the city on 8 May 2008. TWM began to receive batches of Wright Eclipse Gemini-bodied Volvo B7TL from 2003, with this example later transferred to Birmingham and still in use during 2023.

On the same day Alexander ALX400-bodied Dennis Trident 4209 (Y816 TOH) was caught departing Pool Meadow bus station clearly showing Coventry's version of TWM livery. Part of a batch of 100 these were the last to carry registrations under the previous system, most of which did not match with the fleet numbers.

Alexander ALX200-bodied Volvo B6RLE 31321 (P321 JND) was part of a large batch of similar buses originally based at Stagecoach depots around Manchester. A significant number were transferred to Warwickshire garages by the mid-2000s, Rugby in this case, where they were joined by examples which originated with Citybus in Hong Kong. Its step-free entrance would be appreciated by those boarding at Trinity Street, Coventry, on 10 June 2008 whilst performing a short working before its return journey home.

Travel De Courcey Leyland National 2 GHB 221W was caught laying over on Station Terrace in Rugby adjacent to the MRS depot. Numbered 221 when new to Merthyr Tydfil Corporation, its original livery had only been slightly adapted by its new owner. The company ran a number of Warwickshire County Council contracted services, many retaining the old Midland Red route numbering system, with the 580 reaching Coventry via numerous villages in between. (Author's collection)

Route 585 also operated between Rugby and Coventry for which Travel De Courcey MCV Evolution-bodied MAN 556 (AE06 OPH) carried route branding. On 8 May 2008 the vehicle was viewed with a sister vehicle at North Street, Rugby. Travel De Courcey ceased operations in 2020, with Travel Coventry now operating most of their contracts.

In 1999 TWM launched eleven Mercedes-Benz 0405GN integral bendy-buses in Birmingham, with Coventry receiving ten largely similar vehicles in 2003. 6020 (BJ03 ETK) was snaking its way around Broadgate on 8 May 2008, an area now pedestrianised. The bendy-bus era would manage another decade, ending in March 2018.

From 1998 TWM introduced the Mercedes-Benz 0405N integral single-deck vehicle to many of its depots. Viewed on Coventry High Street, the same day as its 'bendy' stablemate, 1569 (S569 VUK) was working route 30 in the clockwise direction. The circular section of the route only applied to the north-east area of the city with Walsgrave Hospital in effect the outer terminus.

Warwickshire County Council used a bold yellow and green livery on vehicles supplied to contractors for use on County Links tendered services. Laying over in Upper Parade on 8 March 2010 was Optare Versa YJ09 EZP, branded for route 68 in Leamington. This was one of five leased to Stagecoach where it was numbered 25241.From the council's own fleet Irizar S-kool-bodied Scania K941B YN54 NYM passes by yet to fill any of its seventy-seat capacity.

Coventry-based Harry Shaw's brightly liveried vehicles have been a familiar sight since 1964 when the company bought its first coach. The handsome lines of the Plaxton Excalibur are shown on T56 MOA, one of a trio with Volvo B10M chassis new in 1999. Viewed on 25 July 2002 in Fairfield Street, beside Manchester Piccadilly Station, decorations were up for the Commonwealth Games taking place in the city at that time. The coach would go on to work for Earlswood Coaches as VIP transport for The Jockey Club, carrying registration SUI 7832. (Author's collection)

The majority of bus routes operated by Johnsons of Henley-in-Arden were contracted with new buses leased to operate them. This included Wright Cadet-bodied DAF SB120 YJ53 VDM soon to embark on a rural ramble from Bridge Street, Stratford-upon-Avon, while the Optare Tempo would remain more local. Both drivers were wearing the company's smart uniform, which complemented the vehicles.

Guide Friday had their depot and headquarters in Stratford-upon-Avon, with several subsequent owners operating from Avenue Farm depot prior to Stagecoach acquiring the business from Ensign Bus in 2006. Shortly afterwards six Northern Counties Paladin-bodied Volvo Olympians new to Cambus were converted to open top for use on the Stratford tour. The circuit, with twelve intermediate stops, began at the Pen & Parchment Inn, Bridgefoot, where on 20 November 2008 16534 (P534 EFL) works the winter timetable with one bus per hour. Transferring within Stagecoach to their operation in the Lake District, the partially open-top vehicle was later sold to Catch 22 for a sightseeing tour of Manchester.

Alexander ALX400-bodied Dennis Trident 18189 (MX54 LPU) had transferred to Stagecoach Warwickshire from Manchester and was working the half-hourly service to Evesham on 19 November 2008. Awaiting custom at Bridge Street in Stratford-upon-Avon two vehicles of this type were regularly allocated to the route.

In April 1994 the Badgerline Group, owners of MRW, invested £3.3 million in thirty-seven Dennis Lance with Plaxton Verde bodywork. Described in publicity as 'British enterprise at work', a further nineteen were delivered during 1995. Initially used to replace Leyland Lynxes based at Digbeth depot, they would later be spread across the whole operating area. 67215 was wearing full 'FG2' livery when loading at Redditch bus station on 17 June 2008 for its hometown of Kidderminster. Some of these vehicles would clock up nearly twenty years' service.

Midland Red 'generations' viewed at Wythall Transport Museum on 8 October 2015. Leyland Titan PD2/12 SHA 431 was one of 100 new to Midland Red in 1953 and bodied by Leyland to a style influenced by MR. Entering preservation in 1971, it would eventually return to the road in 2010. Wright Street Deck 35158 was one of four delivered to Worcester depot in 2015, then part of a much smaller MRW division.

Right at the western edge of our journey, at Gloucester bus station on 28 September 2009, we see Astons of Worcester Optare Solo MX09 AOR on its regular haunt, route 351. At this time the company was owned by French Group Veolia but today is in independent hands. (Raymond Bedford)

The third generation of post-deregulation single-decker used by MRW was introduced in 2005 with thirty-four ADL Enviro 300 following their Dennis Lance and Leyland Lynx predecessors. Initially at Redditch 67649 (VX54 MTK) was later transferred to Worcester where on 1 September 2006 it was loading at the cathedral stop while working to Evesham, in keeping with its window-based route branding.

Warwickshire County Council-owned SN04 EFR was one of a trio of ADL Enviro 300s leased to the contractor of their hourly 'County Links' route X20 between Stratford-upon-Avon and Birmingham for which they were branded. Initially used by Pete's Travel, the bus acquired the identity 403 with its next owner Stratford Blue. When Stagecoach Group acquired that operator in 2006 the bus became 27504, as depicted on 20 November 2008, in Wood Street.

Smith's of Alcester took advantage of deregulation by starting services in Birmingham from late 1987 marketed as Your Bus. Their livery was inspired by Greater Manchester PTE, from where some early vehicle acquisitions were made, and route numbers were suffixed with a 'Y'. Operating to areas south of the city the majority of vehicles were delivered new and featured DAF or Volvo B10M chassis. Representing the latter, 155 was one of eleven with Plaxton Derwent bodywork caught negotiating St Martin's Circus in May 1997. Your Bus was acquired by TWM in 1993 as evidenced by the fleet name above the front grill. After subsequent service with a couple of operators in Scotland the bus is now part of the collection at Wythall Transport Museum. (Kevin Lane/author's collection)

TWM kept the Your Bus identity and applied an orange version of standard fleet livery to vehicles operating within this division. TWM's early low-floor single-deck requirements were met with Volvo's B10L chassis coupled to Wright's stylish Liberator bodywork. 1475 (R475 XDA), from a batch of twenty new in 1997, was loading on a gloomy Edgbaston Street on 23 April 1999. By 2001 members of the Your Bus division were merged into the main fleet and the 'Y' suffix dropped.

The Bull Ring bus station was always gloomy no matter what the weather! Vehicular access was made from Dudley Street and exit onto Edgbaston Street. Closed in 2000 as part of the redevelopment of the Bull Ring Shopping Centre, it was not replaced with just on-street bus stops used thereafter. MRW Leyland Lynx 1144 (G144 HNP) was still able to use the facility on 23 April 1999 working one of a number of routes to destinations south of the city.

During the 1990s United Counties local 'Coachlinks' network included the two-hourly X64 between Corby and Birmingham via several Northamptonshire towns and villages. The majority of the operation ran from Kettering depot where 172 (P172 KBD), a Plaxton Premiere 'Inter-urban'-bodied Volvo B10M, was based. Departing the gloom of Greyfriars bus station, Northampton, on 1 September 1997, its terminus would be the Bull Ring bus station.

The Stagecoach Group launched Megabus in 2003, a no-frills coaching product equivalent to those of low-cost airlines with all bookings made via the internet. The majority of National Express contracts operated by Stagecoach Group subsidiaries had ended by 2004/05, allowing the vehicles to be redeployed to the expanding Megabus network. Jonckheere Mistral 50-bodied Volvo B10M S459 BCE was new to Cambus as 459 in 1998 operating from Peterborough. Later allocated to Rugby as 52619, it was laying over at Dudley Street bus stand on 13 February 2009 before returning to London. One further transfer would soon take place to Stagecoach South, where it would carry 'Southdown' cherished mark 413 DCD.

Following the takeover of Diamond Bus by the Rotala Group in 2008 significant expansion would soon begin across the West Midlands. A large number of contracts were won from Worcestershire County Council, which included the 178 operated from Redditch. On 19 November 2008 Wright Eclipse Urban-bodied Volvo B7RLE 853 was working the service when viewed at Smallbrook Queensway, once a major thoroughfare. The vehicle's branding applied to some of the commercial routes that were launched in Redditch from August 2008.

TWM also favoured the Wright Eclipse Urban-bodied Volvo B7RLE as evidenced by 1787 (BX56 XDJ) on display at Showbus, Duxford, in 2007. Delivered in February that year, it would serve the West Midlands from Acocks Green and Walsall depots. A subsequent transfer within the National Express Group would take it to Travel Dundee, receiving the green Xplore Dundee livery.

TWM took a liking to the Mercedes-Benz 0405N integral single-deck bus with nearly 200 examples operated, making them the UK's largest user of the type. 1587 (S587 VUK) at Dudley bus station on 27 March 2002 1587 (S587 VUK) displays the 'M' logo beside its front destination blind, denoting connections could be made along the route with Midland Metro.

MRN rolled out this traditional livery across the majority of its fleet following application on a handful of vehicles. 1918 (G918 LHA), later renumbered 3148, was one of four East Lancs-bodied Leyland Olympians new in December 1989 that carried this livery between 1993 and 1995. As stated on the clear white-on-blue destination blinds, it was working the main trunk route to Tamworth when seen on Corporation Street in Birmingham. Nothing would remain permanent along this way, with all the bus types depicted now a distant memory and New Street completely pedestrianised. Today the only form of public transport to traverse this junction are the trams of Midland Metro. After subsequent service in Merseyside and Burnley the bus is now preserved in this livery. (Author's collection)

From 1999 TWM began to receive large numbers of Plaxton President-bodied Volvo B7TLs as low-floor replacements for the significant number of MCW Metrobuses in their fleet. 4092 (V92 MOA), based at Yardley Wood depot, wears what would become standard livery, termed 'Connector' in a move away from older blue-based colour schemes. It had received ALX400-sytle front lights when caught laying over at Moat Lane beside Birmingham Markets on 20 November 2008. A subsequent life in Dundee would beckon.

Pete's Travel of West Bromwich was established in May 1993, building up a sizeable fleet by the early 2000s covering much of the West Midlands. Vehicles wore a livery of overall yellow with a significant number leased from Dawson Rentals, those examples identifiable by being registered in Northampton. Plaxton Beaver 2-bodied Mercedes-Benz Vario 0814 T462 HNH was numbered 60 and viewed at Wolverhampton bus station on 9 February 2000. The company, later renamed People's Express, was sold to the Go-Ahead Group in 2006. (Jeff Jones)

On 10 August 1994 Central Coachways (part of TWM) Plaxton Expressliner 2-bodied Volvo B10M K3 CEN was seen at the same location loading passengers for a 'Rapide' journey to London. At that time a handful of journeys ran between the two locations, with a standard return fare of £12 and a hostess service offered. Later re-registered K659 BOH, it, and the three others of the batch, went on extended loan to The Birmingham Coach Company along with the National Express contracts. (Jeff Jones)

The Birmingham Coach Company also operated a large bus fleet from its Tividale depot. Their substantial fleet of Leyland Nationals was joined in 2000 by twenty-four Northern Counties Paladin-bodied Dennis Lance from Metroline. New in 1993, they had formed London Buses LN class based at depots across North West London, the Manchester registrations originated with the bodybuilder. All retained their thirty-seven-seat dual-door layout and received 'Diamond Route' fleet names, which Birmingham County Council applied to certain services. K304 YJA, later numbered 304, was loading at Dudley bus station on 27 March 2002.

The Go-Ahead Group acquired BCC in December 2005 and Pete's Travel in March 2006, renaming the combined 230-vehicle operation Go West Midlands, managed under the control of the Oxford Bus Company. Vehicles were transferred from most Go-Ahead Group companies to replace older inherited stock but by early 2008 the whole operation was sold to the Rotala Group. A considerable number of new vehicles entered service during the first year of their ownership, with this 16 July 2008 view of Tividale depot resembling a dealer's yard! These Volvo B7RLEs await their identities; the Plaxton Centro would receive Black Diamond branding whilst its Wright Eclipse Urban-bodied neighbour would be painted red for use at Redditch.

Merry Hill shopping and leisure complex was built between 1985 and 1990 on the site of the former Round Oak steelworks near Dudley. Initially a monorail operated around the site and an in-house fleet of minibuses ran to destinations in the local area. Other operators would also serve the facility, such as Metropolitan Omnibus of Darlaston, an unusual member of their fleet seen at the on-site bus station on 1 June 1996. Mercedes-Benz 811D G737 NNS began life as a demonstrator for Wright, seeing use with a number of operators including Ulster Bus. The Nimbus bodywork was later redesigned (see page 33). Acquired from Timeline in 1995, it would later serve with fellow Status Group Company Choice Travel. (Jeff Jones)

Infrastructure improvements along significant 'corridors' were often paired with the launch of low-floor vehicles and bold branding. Exemplifying this was TWM 1469 (R469 XDA), one of twenty Wright Liberator-bodied Volvo B10Ls new in October 1997. Waiting passengers have a new shelter and level access boarding thanks to the raised 'Kassel kerb', while the 'red carpets' outlined the bus stop area to road users. Allocated to Walsall garage when this 10 October 1998 scene was taken, it would also work from Perry Bar before withdrawal in May 2012. (Author's collection)

From 1992 opportunities presented with the opening of the east–west A14 road were explored by National Express service 314. Three return journeys were offered between Birmingham and Cambridge with a total journey time of two hours and thirty-five minutes. On 7 August 1997 Premier Travel 445, a Plaxton Expressliner 2-bodied Volvo B10M, would depart Kettering bus station at 12.55 on a westbound journey. The livery variation and branding applied to the frequent 011 service between Cambridge and London.

Cambridge Coach Services also sought similar opportunities between the same two cities, launching route 70 on 27 March 1994 with four return journeys. By October 1994 this had developed into route 71 operating between Worcester and Cambridge via Stratford-upon-Avon and Warwick and branded as 'The Heritage Link'. Jointly operated with associated company Rover of Bromsgrove, the route lasted until December 1998. Tours, day trips and private hire work was also undertaken, with Van Hool Alizee-bodied Volvo B10M 345 (D345 KVE) on such duties in Blackpool. (Author's collection)

Redditch-based Hardings are an established firm running tours and private hire work alongside a number of local contracts. Jonckheere Deauville-bodied MAN 16.290 (K4 HCR, K219 CBD), one of a pair acquired from Buddens of Romsey, was far from home on 5 July 2001 when seen at Colon La Rambla in Barcelona.

Diamond S397 HVV was one of a sizeable number of Plaxton Pointer 2-bodied Dennis Dart SLFs used by Pete's Travel. The livery was applied when under Go-Ahead Group ownership, as was the fleet number 426. Loading at Redditch bus station on 17 June 2008 on the busy Matchborough service, the laminated A board signified a journey via Queen Alexandra Hospital.

Johnsons' smartly presented Optare Tempo YJ07 EHH, one of a pair, was descending Station Way and about to enter Redditch bus station on 17 June 2008. The 'Excelbus' brand was applied to Johnsons bus services. This side of their business would eventually be sold to Rotala Group in April 2022.

Rotala's Redditch depot received eleven Wright Eclipse Urban-bodied Volvo B7RLEs for services around the town. Branded Red Diamond, their livery was reminiscent of Midland Red whose former depot forms the backdrop to this view. Go-Ahead brought this site back into use and Rotala would eventually vacate it when they acquired First's depot and operations in the town. A press launch took place on 18 July 2008 with 852 running on trade plates for the day, the identity BU08 DBV applied later.

Smart 'mini' single-deck low-floor members of the Diamond fleet at Redditch included this duo seen inside at Church Road depot on 28 July 2008. Acquired from OFJ Connections, KX57 OWM was a Transbus MPD with ALX200 bodywork numbered 517, which regularly worked commercial route 51 to Batchley. Its older stablemate was Plaxton Pointer 2-bodied Dennis Dart SLF 518 (KU02 YUA) previously with Jones of Llanfaethlu. Both were awaiting application of fleet names and vinyl graphics.

Leyland National 544 was new to Midland Red's Worcester depot in September 1976, serving the city and surrounding area until withdrawal in December 1995. In early 1997 it was sold to the Wythall Transport Museum where it was viewed on 8 October 2015 in MRW's post-privatisation livery.

The National Exhibition Centre is located adjacent to Birmingham International Airport and hosts a wide variety of exhibitions, events and entertainment including the bus and coach industry's annual trade show. From 2006 National Express began to specify the wheelchair-accessible Caetano Levante for its contractors coupled to Volvo or Scania chassis. The model had been launched in late 2005 by the Portuguese manufacturer and featured a wheelchair lift and 'magic floor' to accommodate all passengers in a 'traditional' layout via the front entrance.

A rather different product was demonstrated at the 1988 event in the shape of the high-specification Van Hool Astral with Volvo B10MT chassis. Belonging to Len Wright Band Services, who offered specialised VIP transport for bands and their entourage, F68 SMC wore their distinctive livery and carried the name 'Gold II'. (Author's collection)

Traditional UK bus and coach manufacturers saw increased competition from European products from the late 1970s. By offering UK-built chassis to European bodybuilders it was hoped some share of the market could be kept. One such example was this Jonckheere Jubilee P50-bodied Leyland Tiger, which, when new, was used by Leyland as a demonstrator. When this June 1984 view was taken it was owned by Smiths Imperial Coachways of Birmingham, serving faithfully with them until the company closed in 2001. (Author's collection)

The smart lines of the Plaxton Paramount 3200 featured on UMO 58, a Volvo B10M owned by NN Cresswell of Evesham. Still wearing the colours of its previous owner, Machins of Ashby de la Zouch, it lays over on Victoria Street on a visit to Northampton on 8 April 1998. That town's main market days were Wednesday and Saturday and trips to nearby Althorpe House were very popular at this time.

Interesting vehicles were a feature of the Geoff Amos fleet and in the early 2000s a number of Leyland Olympians were acquired from Isle of Man Transport. Those which had previously operated on the mainland regained their old registration marks including ECW-bodied 102 A682 KDV, one of a pair acquired in 2001, which carried the identity MAN 55N on IoM. New to Devon General then Southern National, this was the first time the vehicle had not been based in a coastal area. Recorded at its new owner's main depot, Woodford service station, it had still to receive a new destination blind and Amos' livery. The identity HIL 6812 would later be applied and the bus remained with the company until their closure in 2011. (Author's collection)

Jeffs Head Office was an old railway station serving the village of Helmdon, near Brackley, where, on 20 April 2002, Beulas Stergo e-bodied Iveco Euro Rider Y809 YBC was seen laying over between duties. The company was sold to the Bowens Group in December 2004 and remained under their control until the group closed in October 2012.

Bowens Group also owned Northampton-based Yorks Coaches where a number of vehicles received Bowens livery. This included Van Hool-bodied Volvo B10M 89 (387 TYD, E263 OMT) which was acquired from Travellers of Hounslow in 1994. It was caught while taking a break after its morning school duties at St Gregory's Road in Northampton on 17 March 1998.

First Northampton maintained a small fleet of coaches for private hire and contract work with a separate rota of drivers to operate them. On 18 July 2004 Plaxton Paramount 3500-bodied Volvo B10M 20037, previously numbered 11, was loading at Chiltern Way in Northampton for a day on the south coast.

The Grand Tourer luxury brand had been launched by Wallace Arnold in 2005 and retained after that organisation merged with Shearings. Making a comfort stop at Watford Gap services on 28 June 2009 was brand-new BK09 RMU, an integrally built Setra S416GT-HD with forty-eight seats. This service area was the first to be opened on the M1, a local theatre group performing *Watford Gap the Musical* to celebrate its fiftieth birthday that year.

Loughborough-based Paul. S. Winson operate a fleet of very well-presented vehicles, many of which feature auxiliary fittings and 'finishing touches' as detailed on BW04 PSW. The Jonckheere Mistral 50-bodied Volvo B12B represented the company in 2004 and 2005 at the Showbus rally held at Duxford.

Skills of Nottingham FC04 LDA, later SIL 6436, was of similar vintage, chassis and body type to the last image and one of a pair new to Irish operator Callinan, Claregedway, in April 2004. Both were acquired by Skills in March 2007, with this example previously registered 04-G-5403. It was seen taking a break at Watford Gap services on 28 June 2009.

A number of cross-country routes were introduced by Megabus, linking major centres without running via London. The M34 ran from Portsmouth and Southampton to destinations in the Midlands and north of England. The calling point at Oxford was originally Water Eaton P&R site where on 2 April 2011 52526 was seen while heading north. The coach was allocated to Rugby depot with a Portsmouth-based driver working this section of the route as far as Birmingham Airport. The Plaxton Paragon-bodied Volvo B10M was new to Yorkshire Traction in 2001 for National Express contracts numbered 66 and carrying the identity 1737 HE. It would later become a driver training vehicle.

Eleven new tri-axle Volvo B12Bs were delivered to Rugby depot in mid-2009 featuring Plaxton Panther bodywork with sixty-three seats, wheelchair lift and accommodation for one wheelchair user. 54054 (KX09 NCN) had yet to enter service in this 2 August 2009 view inside Rugby depot where driver familiarisation was being conducted at the time. Despite their 15-metre length and large 'P45' mirrors, the vehicles were very manoeuvrable and offered considerable space for passengers' luggage. The latter was not a common feature on the double-deck vehicles in use on the Scottish cross-border services which required the addition of a luggage trailer as seen in the distance. Passengers and road users in the UK and North America alike became familiar with the image of 'Sid', who also had a strong following on social media!

Taking their name from founder Frank Flight, the Birmingham-based company saw rapid development through the 1970s, which included, most appropriately, daily services to a number of UK airports. Impressive double-deck vehicles featured on these routes including Van Hool Astron TOA 717Y, viewed in May 1985 departing Heathrow Terminal 2. The coach would subsequently work for Redfern of Mansfield, receiving the registration GIL 3206. Flights' airport services were later taken over by the Flightlink division of National Express. (Author's collection)

With operations initially based in Nottinghamshire, Dunn Line expanded by acquiring several companies in the northern 'Home Counties'. After a period owned by Veolia, Dunn Line reacquired the business, branding the operations as Your Bus. National Express contracts featured throughout as exemplified by Caetano Levante-bodied Volvo B12B 4104 (FJ56 PBY) loading at St Margaret's bus station in Leicester on 28 April 2008 on a working between Stansted and Nottingham.

Arriva Midlands provided a local link to East Midlands Airport from Leicester where Wright Eclipse-bodied Volvo B7L 3613 (SA02 CCV) was viewed on 28 April 2008. One of a pair acquired from Whitelaws of Stonehouse in 2005, they joined a similar example in the fleet with all featuring additional luggage racks and dedicated route branding. The bus returned to Scotland in 2009 when acquired by McGills.

After the Second World War Elmdon Airport was developed to offer commercial flights and renamed Birmingham International Airport. TWM operated half-hourly route 900 between Birmingham and Coventry via the airport with a total journey time of one hour. This wasn't a twenty-hour-hour service but it was limited stop, including Allison Street at Digbeth where 4633 (BX54 XSA), a Transbus Trident with ALX400 body, picks up a good load on 20 November 2008. Today Platinum service X1 covers much the same route up to every twenty minutes twenty-four hours a day.

Warwickshire County Council's County Links contracted services included connections to Birmingham Airport from Atherstone (777) or Nuneaton (717), each on an hourly headway. Five Scania Omnicity integral vehicles were used on the routes which were operated by Stagecoach Warwickshire. The last of the Nuneaton-based batch YN56 NNG, numbered 28505, was loading at that town's bus station on 8 May 2008. The bus would see subsequent use with Johnsons of Henley-in-Arden and Trustybus in Harlow.

Geoff Amos' principal bus service ran between Banbury and Rugby loosely following the route of the Great Central Railway and was later marketed as 'The Great Central Connection'. Some unusual vehicles were used in an equally unusual livery of cream and purple. Plaxton Supreme-bodied Bedford XNH 119S was passing Rugby 'Midland' station on 29 June 1987 from a time when the frequency was roughly every two hours and only a few journeys ran its full length. (Kevin Lane)

Amos 53 (AM05 BUS) was laying over in Banbury on 24 November 2009 and offered a very different product to that of the previous picture. The service was increased to provide an hourly headway over the full length of the route and low-floor vehicles were introduced in 2000. Following the closure of the company in 2011 the MCV Evolution-bodied MAN, along with its cherished registration, went to Faresaver of Chippenham. (Raymond Bedford)

Red bricks, red telephone boxes and red route branding feature in this 23 December 2001 view outside Leicester railway station, with the bus working a replacement service to Market Harborough and Kettering on behalf of Midland Mainline. Between 1997 and 1999 twenty-four Wright Access Floline-bodied Scanias were shared between First Leicester and Northampton, with a further four acquired in 2000 from First Leeds. The quartet was allocated to Northampton including 365 (S101 CSG), previously numbered 8101 in Yorkshire and later receiving national series number 61137 when transferred to First Manchester.

Following deregulation, a wave of corporate colour schemes swept away many traditional liveries. Derby City Transport changed their corporate colours several times pre- and post-privatisation with the two-tone blue scheme, introduced with one-man operation, replacing that of original olive green and cream. Volvo products were favoured by the company with the double-deck Ailsa followed by the Citybus, as exemplified by 151 (E151 BTO), one of five with Northern Counties bodywork new in 1988. Seen at Derby Midland station on 26 July 1995, it would soon receive the red, yellow and blue 'City Rider' scheme. It would finally wear an Arriva corporate coat, becoming part of the Midlands division as 4351. (Jeff Jones)

Fraser Eagle organised a considerable amount of rail replacement work during the early 2000s and distributed it to contractors, their bright day-glo signage displayed in the windscreen of Leyland National 2 LUI 7665. New to NCT as B718 LAL, the bus, owned by Premiere Travel, stands beside railway premises in Station Street, Nottingham, on 19 February 2005.

NCT had received a batch of early-production Leyland Nationals in 1973, with some of their fleet numbers reissued to members of the mark 2 version which began arriving from 1980. 714, part of the 1985 batch, eases from Middle Hill to Canal Street in August 1992 overlooked by the bridge which once carried the Great Central Railway (GCR) through the city, part of which had, by then, been permanently severed. (Kevin Lane)

Nottingham Express Transit (NET) opened in March 2004, bringing trams back to the streets of Nottingham. Fifteen Derby-built Bombardier Incentro units were initially used, numbered 201 to 215, with each unit formed of five articulated sections. Station Street was the original city terminus located upon part of the old GCR bridge where one of the units was viewed on 19 February 2005. The 'severed' part of the bridge was rebuilt at a later date when the NET network expanded, thus making this a through station.

Stagecoach Group operated the South West Trains and East Midlands Trains rail franchises along with a 49 per cent share of Virgin Trains. Opportunities were sought to integrate parts of these operations, with the bus division Megabus Plus being one such venture. The trio of coach routes, which served the East Midlands, Humberside and parts of Yorkshire, were in effect feeder services to East Midlands Parkway where passengers changed to a specific rail departure for St Pancras. The launch day was 12 April 2009, which unfortunately coincided with engineering works leading to all three coaches running through to London with no train ride! Hull-based Jonckheere Mistral-bodied Volvo B10M 52490 awaits its northbound passengers at St Pancras bus station.

MCW Metrobus 2883 (B883 DOM), new in 1985, was still wearing an older version of TWM livery when travelling along Albert Street in the city centre on 19 November 2008. Part of the original Curzon Street station and The Woodman pub, behind the bus, remain the only survivors of a previous era at this location. The same could not be said for Spanish restaurant Los Canarios or Rosa's Café, two well-loved venues, located behind the photographer, since demolished. Bus services now take a different path and the area to the right will (eventually) become the midlands terminus of HS2.

During the 1980s and 1990s Stevensons of Uttoxeter operated a fascinating fleet that contained many unique vehicles including ECW-bodied Leyland Olympian 99 (Q246 FVT). Built to dual-door configuration in 1979, the unregistered Leyland test rig joined Stevensons in 1983 without seats. The bus gained the more unusual Q-registration in place of a yearly 'V' or 'A' mark. Such plates were something of a rarity, although perhaps not with this operator! MCW Metrobus 80 (TOJ 592S), parked in the next row back, was also a significant vehicle. New in 1977 as a demonstrator for MCW, this was the forerunner to over 4,000 of the type built at Washwood Heath in Birmingham. A considerable fleet of Metrobuses would be operated as evidenced in this scene at Burton-upon-Trent depot in May 1993. (Author's collection)

The blue and silver livery of TWM dominates this 23 April 1999 scene in Edgbaston Street, with Lea Hall's 3082 (F82 XOF) loading for an 'anti-clockwise' trip of the 590.

The conversion from step entrance to low-floor vehicles in Birmingham took a more gradual pace than London where continual large-scale withdrawal would see most step entrance buses removed in just over five years. Operators such as Coastal Liner took the opportunity to add such vehicles to their fleets, with MCW Metrobus GYE 403W acquired from Metroline. Promotional advertising is displayed over paintwork which originated with London Buses. TWM's route numbers were also applied by numerous private operators in the West Midlands as can be seen at Dudley bus station on 27 March 2002 on a service that the incumbent operator ran up to every twelve minutes.

3001 (F301 XOF) smartly carried an older version of TWM livery as applied to Coventry-based vehicles as it heads through its home city on 8 May 2008. TWM's final Metrobuses were withdrawn from Coventry mid-2010.

Between 1995 and 1999 Marshall of Cambridge refurbished over 600 of TWM's Metrobuses, which included structural work. This was most noticeable at the rear with a smaller back window installed, as detailed on this preserved duo at Showbus, Duxford, in 2011. 2462 (NOA 462X) with original styling carries a more traditional livery than refurbished 2618 (ROX 618Y), last used at Coventry.

Scania products proved popular in Leicester, with both Leicester Citybus and Midland Fox operating numerous examples. Midland Fox acquired a number of second-hand vehicles, which, in 1993, included six Alexander RH-bodied N113DRB from BTS of Borehamwood. Loading at Haymarket for Oadby Grange on 18 January 1994, 4156 (F156 DET) still displays its external running number holder but had yet to receive a new destination blind. (Jeff Jones)

Arriva Midlands 4176 (M176 GRY) was one of twenty Scania N113 DRB new to Midland Fox in 1994, their East Lancs bodywork to a similar style as Alexander. Viewed at Belgrave Gate in Leicester on 28 April 2008, it would soon transfer, along with several others, to Arriva North East, this example becoming 7262.

A P&R scheme was introduced in Shrewsbury in November 1994 and a unified livery was applied by contractors operating the services. In April 1995 four East Lancs-bodied Scania MaxCi were delivered to MRN, with 1402, later 3502, seen working the route to Meole Brace devoid of branding. The quartet served the town until 2011, with this example seeing subsequent service with JPT of Middleton, Greater Manchester. (Author's collection)

The low-floor Scania MaxCi didn't prove popular in the UK. Only a dozen examples were built, with operators ordering step-entrance vehicles for a while longer. Arriva Midlands 2179, later 3479, (N179 PUT) was the last of a batch of fourteen East Lancs European-bodied Scania L113CRL new to Midland Fox in 1996. Dual-purpose seating and Arriva's 'inter-urban' colours featured when seen at St Margaret's bus station on 8 May 2008.

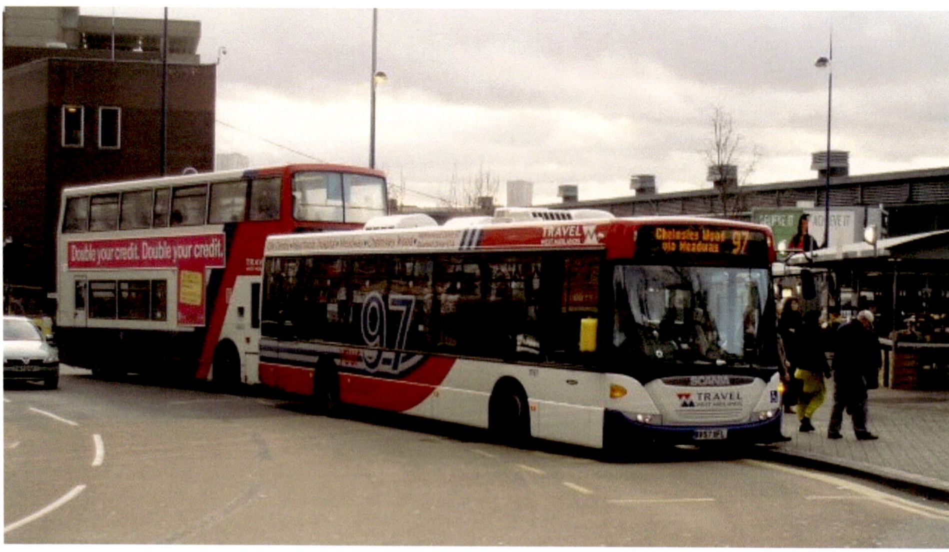

TWM and its predecessors only operated one Metro-Scania single-deck vehicle from 1972 and a batch of Alexander-bodied Scania double-deck vehicles, which entered service in 1990. The integral Scania Omnilink would prove more popular, with 165 units being delivered between 2007 and 2010. 1797 (BV57 XFL) unloads at Birmingham Markets on 20 November 2008 and carried branding for high-frequency route 'Your 97', not connected to erstwhile Your Bus. During its fifteen-year career with TWM the bus would work from six of their depots.

Numbered 5, B505 PRF was one of nine Dormobile-bodied Ford Transits new in 1985 to MRN Stafford depot. By 1989 the sixteen-seater had moved to Derby where it was used on services competing with Derby City Transport. This included route A1 to Alveston with a few passengers boarding at the city's Market Place. In retaliation Derby set up routes in Tamworth, operating them with Volvo Citybuses. (Author's collection)

By 1990 the competitive routes of both operators had ceased, with MRN selling several minibuses to Derby City Transport in the process. Some were acquired from other sources such as C467 BHY, a Dormobile-bodied Ford Transit previously numbered 7467 at Bristol. (Author's collection)

Following deregulation Leicester Citybus looked to expand beyond the city boundary and set up operations in Loughborough and Stamford. Loughborough Bus & Coach Company traded as 'Trippet' on routes around that town which had been withdrawn by Barton. Fifteen smart Optare Citypacers were used, four of which were loading together in the town centre. After only a short period the routes passed to Midland Fox and the vehicles to Derby City Transport. (Author's collection)

The majority of early minibus designs clearly gave away their van heritage with a very 'cosy' feel to their saloons. Coach-type seating added some appeal and presented opportunities for private hire. NCT received fifteen Reeve Burgess-bodied Renault-Dodge minibuses in 1987, with the last three of the batch fitted with twenty-five coach seats and painted in the orange and brown coach livery. 133 was caught entering Canal Street in August 1992 while working a local service. The bus would see subsequent use locally with Dunn-Line and NCT's more stylish Optare Solos would later reuse the fleet number series. (Kevin Lane)

Later minibus designs were more stylish and gave an almost 'big bus' feel. Mercedes-Benz had great success in the minibus market from deregulation up to the beginning of the low-floor era, and their Vario product was chosen by Midland Fox to be their last 'cubs'. Only 150 of the ALX100 model were built by Alexander between 1997 and 1999, with Midland Fox taking twenty-five. The final livery style prior to Arriva corporate colours was shown on 101, later numbered 1101, when exhibited at Showbus, Duxford, on 21 September 1997.

Plaxton's Beaver 2 bodywork was more commonly coupled to the Vario as exemplified by YN54 WCY belonging to Woods of Wigston. Working one of the Market Harborough town services at the Square on 3 June 2008, both the bus and the route would later pass to Centrebus.

Centrebus was one of a number of operators to benefit from the large numbers of step-entrance midibuses displaced from London. Established service 54 operated for a number of years against the LCB route of the same number, with most journeys running to Goodwood. On 28 April 2008 Plaxton Pointer-bodied Dennis Dart P35MLE, acquired from Armchair in 2002, was operating one of several journeys on the route, which extended to Loughborough.

Much variety was on offer at Abbey Park Road depot on 20 April 2003. Dennis Falcon-HC 622 carried the experimental green, white and yellow scheme on its Northern Counties Paladin bodywork. 424, of similar appearance, was one of several Volvo B6s acquired from First Capital in 2000 and wears standard 'FG2' livery. Its former East London stablemate, Plaxton Pointer-bodied Dennis Dart 693 (K903 CVW), still wore First Capital livery and their fleet number. Outstationed by Kinch Bus was 808 (M808 PRA), an unusual Optare Vecta-bodied MAN new to parent company Trent. Northern Counties Paladin-bodied Volvo B6 432 (L5 GML) completes the line up, its experimental livery lacking the yellow waistband.

Introduced in 1998, the Solo from Optare was a popular choice for operators seeking a low-floor replacement for minibuses or midibuses. Stagecoach Group introduced the type to Preston and Leamington Spa in 2001. By 8 May 2008 47010 (KX51 CTE), from the initial batch, loads at stand 14 in Nuneaton bus station. 'Network Nuneaton' branded 47069 (KN04 XKC), named *Larry Grayson* manoeuvres around the facility where roadways are lettered and bays numbered.

Ironically, from the turn of the new millennium the design of many new minibus models seemed to revert to a more van-like styling. Judges of Corby operated this accessible Rohill Harrier-bodied Renault Master on county council contracts such as the 167, viewed at Market Hall in Market Harborough on 3 June 2008.

Under First Group ownership numerous inter-company transfers took place, with LCB receiving several Leyland Lynxes. F602 RTC was viewed at Belmont Gate on 28 April 2008 with National series number 62602. The vehicle was new to Bristol Omnibus, pioneers of the 'Over Ground' brand, which was inherited by First and applied to a number of their constituent companies.

The option to rebody older vehicles became common post-deregulation, with a number of manufacturers offering such conversions. The Willowbrook Warrior was of similar appearance to the Lynx; Kinch operated a trio with Leyland Leopard chassis. New as a coach to Northern General with Willowbrook 003 bodywork, 471 (HIL 7771, TUP 582V) was rebodied in 1991. The company ran a number of routes in Nottingham where the bus was caught departing Broadmarsh bus station on 18 January 1994. Perhaps the rather stern looking passenger would have preferred a Lynx! (Jeff Jones)

Inter-company transfers or loans were common as needs dictated or operations acquired. This is exemplified by Midland Fox 3490 (JOX 490P), which joined the Loughborough Bus & Coach division in May 1989. Loading for Loughborough in Haymarket, Leicester, on 18 January 1994, an 'On hire to Kinch Bus' sign is displayed in the windscreen. Later in 1994 the bus would transfer within the British Bus Group to Guildford and West Surrey after being rebodied as an East Lancs Greenway and re-registered PDZ 6273. DRM of Bromyard acquired the bus in July 2003 giving it the identity MOI 9565. It remained with that operator until being scrapped in April 2009. (Jeff Jones)

Yellow-liveried vehicles would remain a feature of the route with Kinch Bus Plaxton Pointer-bodied Dennis Dart SLF 896 (P408 BNR) departing St Margaret's bus station on 8 May 2008. One of five new in September 1996 the series 8xx was used by parent Trent Barton to identify vehicles of the Kinch Bus division.

Barton Transport was acquired by the Wellglade Group in 1989, initially being run as a separate unit, vehicles numbered in the series 1xxx and the Robin Hood logo retained. 1605 (VRC 605Y) was one of nine late model Leyland Leopards with Plaxton Supreme IV bodywork. An additional luggage rack had been fitted behind the driver when this 18 January 1994 view was taken at Broadmarsh bus station. (Jeff Jones)

Stevensons varied fleet features once more at Burton-upon-Trent. Willowbrook 003-bodied Leyland Leopard 137 (LOA 834X) was one of a pair acquired from Victoria Motorways of Woodville in 1987. Both were sold to Motts Travel of Stoke Mandeville in March 1992, joining their appropriately named 'Yellow Bus' division. Loading behind was Alexander RH-bodied MCW Metrobus 73 (UWW 512X), new to West Yorkshire PTE as 7512 and one of four acquired from that source in 1987. (Author's collection)

The long-established Vivtoria/Viking business was acquired by Stevensons who retained their two-tone grey livery and fleet names. The company operated a programme of holiday express services from locations across the Midlands to a great number of costal resorts. Plaxton Paramount 3200-bodied Volvo B10M 25, new in 1989, was seen when new at that year's Showbus rally held at Woburn Abbey. (Author's collection)

A busy scene on Edgbaston Street on 23 April 1999 with TWM's 2754 finding space to pick up its Lea Hall-bound passengers. MRN 1747 was one of four Alexander N-bodied Leyland Tigers acquired from Timeline in 1993, later followed by a further ten of the Belfast-style batch. Their high capacity was useful on busy trunk routes such as the 110 to Tamworth, which was usually operated by double-deckers. Motts Travel acquired six of this batch from Arriva Midlands in 2002.

Felix of Ilkeston operated a number of bus services alongside their coaching business, their name inspired by cartoon character Felix the cat. Examples of Leyland's 'cats' were recorded at the company's Station Road depot led by Plaxton Derwent-bodied Leyland Tiger F697 HNU ahead of a trio of former Arriva Yorkshire Lynxes. The feline-association would remain with the principal route to Derby, being marketed as 'The Black Cat' in later years. (Author's collection)

At the most northerly part of our journey we meet the operations of Hulleys, who are based in the Peak District village of Baslow. A more standard fleet was operated by the early 2000s, including eight Leyland Lynxes as exemplified by F289 AWW and G193 EOG, which were acquired from Arriva Yorkshire and TWM respectively. The pair were bookended by more unusual M802 PRA, an Optare Vecta-bodied MAN acquired from Trent, and Plaxton Verde-bodied Dennis Lance (P659 BUB) new to Longstaff of Mirfield and registered P2 JLL. (Author's collection)

Leyland National 432 (KVO 432P) was waiting to load at Derby's old bus station displaying Trent Buses fleet names and showing a Barton slip-board in the windscreen. Many of this large batch of the type received internal refurbishment, making them appealing on the second-hand market when replaced by new vehicles, this example being sold to Hi-Ride of Smethwick. (Author's collection)

Derby's 142 was the penultimate example from a batch of ten Citybuses new in 1984, which carried unusual and rather tall-looking Marshall bodywork. Suitably large lettering featured on the side of the bus, which was on display at the Showbus rally held at Woburn Abbey in September 1989. Two months prior a consortium of managers, employees and Luton & District had bought the company from the council. Its neighbour that day, WMT, would undergo such a management buyout two years later. Derby would eventually become part of Arriva and WMT the National Express Group. (Author's collection)

From the mid-1960s until 1989 NCT specified its own unique design to manufacturers of its double-deck vehicles, giving them a 'standard' look. The majority were paired to the Leyland Atlantean chassis but in later years other types would feature. Vehicles 'on trial' were generally numbered at the end of a sequence x98 or x99 as exemplified on 399, one of a pair of East Lancs-bodied Volvo B10M 'Citybuses' new in 1983. Their trial was against the comparable Leyland Olympian and Dennis Falcon types with Volvo proving most successful. Working towards Bulwell in August 1992 the bus had just entered Market Street, a roadway now used by trams. (Kevin Lane)

Trent began replacing its fleet soon after privatisation with twenty-four Alexander RV-bodied Volvo Citybuses delivered between 1988 and 1990. Numerically first 600 (F600 GVO) was allocated to Hucknell Garage and used primarily on the Mansfield to Nottingham service, upon which it was viewed departing Broadmarsh bus station on 19 April 1994. All would be sold after a decade of service and no further double-deckers were received. This example went with several others to Plymouth Citybus, after which it headed north to Wigan Coachways and Diamond Bus in the north-west. In 2016 it was acquired for preservation by Mark Butler and is now part of the Nottingham Heritage Vehicle collection. (Jeff Jones)

NCT's distinctive styling and smart livery is carried on East Lancs-bodied Leyland Atlantean 624 (MNU 624P) travelling along Milton Street, returning from Gedling, on 19 April 1994. A considerable number of the type were still in use at this time, with their eventual replacements carrying 'off the peg' styling and single-door configuration. (Jeff Jones)

NCT operated a central circuit that linked several significant city centre locations and was branded 'Cityline'. Leyland National 2s were regularly allocated to the service, with many carrying all-over adverts such as well-laden 706 caught in Angel Row. In subsequent years Dunn Line would operate the service. (Kevin Lane)

Having sold their bus and coach operations to Veolia in 2006 Dunn Line would return to Nottinghamshire once more when 'Your Bus' was launched in May 2009. A series of local routes was built up and a number of National Express contracts gained. Recorded in Retford on 28 June 2010 was 2506 (X701 EGK), one of six Dennis Tridents with handsome Plaxton President bodywork acquired from London General. This example was previously numbered PDL10 at Stockwell Garage and its time in the Metropolis was captured in the background of a promotional poster for the film *South Kensington*. By October 2019 Your Bus had closed with many of the vehicles transferred to Diamond Bus, Preston, in this case, where it received the identity 40011. (Author's collection)

The 'off the peg' styling featured on a batch of thirty-two Dennis Tridents with East Lancs Lolyne bodywork, which NCT's livery suited very well. Laying over on Angel Row on 18 February 2001, 424 (V424 DRC) was a longstanding member of the fleet and later received the red version of 'Go-2' livery.

In 1993/4 Trent received twenty-eight Northern Counties Paladin-bodied Volvo B10Bs registered in the series L-LRA. A further ten 'M' registered examples would be received and all would operate on the quality 'Rainbow routes' alongside the equally smart vehicles bodied by Optare. On 19 April 1994 114 (L114 LRA) was leading a procession of interesting cars along Milton Street in Nottingham – the bus is far newer than any of them! (Jeff Jones)

NCT body styling was also applied to a small batch of Roe-bodied Leyland Atlanteans new in 1981. Loading on Carrington Street in April 1991, 479 (NNN 479W) was at the over-bridge carrying it over Station Street. The bus would subsequently see use with Paul. S. Winson in Loughborough and later in a non-PCV role at Cribbs Causeway with Young Driver.eu. The bus is now preserved and a Brit Bus model of the vehicle also exists. The iron roads of NET now also reach the suburb of Clifton. (Kevin Lane)

Leyland National 2 BVP 814V was new to Midland Red at Cannock in 1980. NCT acquired it in 1988 at a time when it was purchasing second-hand examples of the type to compliment its own. Periods of loan in 1990 saw it operate with Midland Fox and council-owned Northampton Transport viewed with the latter at Greyfriars bus station on 9 November 1990. From October 1996 the vehicle operated with Hulleys of Baslow where it lasted five years, surely earning the bus the title of 'Midlands meanderer'. (Author's collection)

In late 1991 Northampton Transport sold four Renault-Dodge S56s with Alexander-AM bodywork to NCT. Retaining their Northampton fleet numbers 103/4/7/8, they featured twenty-three coach seats with 103, named *Rosie* by its previous owner, entering Friar Lane from South Parade when newly acquired. NCT took one more (105) in 1993 and the remaining three moved to Aberdeen during the period Northampton was owned by GRT. After service with Arvonia in North Wales 103 became a mobile home and is still believed to exist in this role. (Kevin Lane)

Sheffield Omnibus acquired eight Bristol VRs from Northampton Transport in 1992, which carried uniquely styled Alexander bodywork. Two of the type, which also saw use in Sheffield, were seen in Milton Street on 19 April 1994 with 1546 (CNH 46T) returning from Arnold. Nottingham Omnibus ran a number of routes against NCT with their vehicles smartly turned out in this Preston-inspired livery. Soon after this scene was captured the company would withdraw from the city to focus on its Sheffield operation, which in turn would later be taken over by Yorkshire Traction. (Jeff Jones)

United Counties for many years provided a route from Nottingham to Northampton via Leicester, which was part of its inter-urban 'Coachlinks' network. By the mid-1990s only one journey per day served destinations north of Leicester on route X61 operated by Northampton depot. In addition Corby depot provided a most unusual journey on Saturdays only. Operating as X63 from Corby to Nottingham via Market Harborough and Leicester, the scheduled return journey departed Nottingham at 12:20 p.m. numbered X61, retracing its path to Corby. ECW-bodied Leyland Olympian 608 is homeward-bound on this journey as it descends Middle Hill beside Broadmarsh bus station. (Author's collection)

Six open-top MCW Metrobuses of West Midlands Travel origin joined the Stagecoach Group through their acquisition of the Traction Group in 2005. Operating from RoadCar's Skegness depot, BLZ 1424 (POG 591Y) carried fleet number 15977 in the Stagecoach scheme having previously been numbered 744 and originally 2591 with WMT. It was wearing an adapted version of corporate livery with locally themed advertising while heading along Grand Parade 22 July 2007 working route 3 to Anchor Lane, with no one 'bracing' the open topper. Dennis Tridents would eventually take over such duties, with this bus scrapped in March 2012 after a career of nearly thirty years.

In order to upgrade their minibus fleet during 1998 MRW received sixty-four Plaxton Beaver 2-bodied Mercedes-Benz Varios. Built with twenty-seven seats, local driver's pay agreement saw them downseated to twenty-two before entering service. First Group were masters of the internal transfer and by 2004 forty-three of the batch had moved south-west. This included 52552 (S552 RWP), new to Worcester depot as 552 and based at Cambourne when caught in the beautiful surroundings of Fowey working evening route 26B to the Lost Gardens of Heligan on 3 June 2008. (Malcolm Crowe)

In 1973 a joint venture by MCW and Scania produced the double-deck Metropolitan. Production ran until 1978 with a total of 660 units being built, significant customers being London Transport (LT) , Leicester City Bus and Reading Transport. Of the 164 vehicles new to LT, all had been withdrawn by the early 1980s with many passing to independent operators. One such example was County Travel of Leicester who took a trio of Metropolitans in 1985 for their County Links local bus services in and around Leicester. Carrying the fleet number 87 with its new owner, along with a detailed set of destination blinds, KJD 278P had been MD78 with LT. In May 1987 it was sold to Rennies of Dunfermline who were keen users of this unusual type with this vehicle being captured in model form by Brit Bus during its time in Scotland. In 1989 the County Links bus routes passed to Midland Fox. The legacy of the Metropolitan was the use of many design features for MCW's Metrobus, which can be seen on pages 68 and 95. (Kevin Lane)

One of fifteen Volvo Olympians new to NCT in 1998 carrying East Lancs Pyoneer bodywork was R480 RRA. Ten Volvo Citybuses of similar appearance were also operated by NCT, the last of the chassis type built. Western Greyhound bought several ex-NCT double-deckers, with the example illustrated becoming their 499 and later re-registered 499 YMK. Laying over in Exeter bus station on 3 June 2008 the vehicle's capacity was required on the busy 510 service linking the city to Newquay via a host of destinations in between. (Malcolm Crowe)

Hulleys of Baslow fleet number 16 was a Bristol RELH6L with ECW bodywork, one of eight new to Trent in 1974. 'Bus Grant' doors featured along with branding for route X67, which linked Mansfield to Liverpool via Manchester. In September 1989 it had travelled south for the day to attend the Showbus rally at Woburn Abbey. (Author's collection)

From October 1986 the operations of Chase Bus Services expanded with the acquisition of numerous county council contracts which took their buses further across Staffordshire, the West Midlands and into Birmingham. Leyland Nationals were introduced from late 1987, a type that would become synonymous with the company, many acquired from Greater Manchester PTE, whose livery was retained by Chase. Marshall-bodied Leyland Leopard number 45, one of seven acquired from MRN, represents one of the old order seen in Cannock during August 1988. Chase would eventually be taken over by Arriva. (Kevin Lane)

To commemorate Midland Red's centenary in 2004 MRS Rugby-based Alexander PS-bodied Volvo B10M 20202 (M202 LHP) received this traditional livery. MRN went one step further by applying registration L100 PHA to Stafford-based Marshall C37-bodied Dennis Dart 2038, the letters 'HA' long-associated with older MR vehicles. The Dart had previously carried another 'select' mark, M30 MPS, when with Mercury Passenger Services of Hoo. The pair were viewed at Nuneaton depot, its architecture similar to a number of other traditional MR depots. The Dart kept a red-based livery with Arriva-owned Wardle Transport and 20202 is now preserved. (Author's collection)

The Routemaster was not a common sight across the Midlands region, only appearing in more recent years for its novelty value. During Ensign-ownership Stratford-upon-Avon depot received RML2565 (JJD 565D) in September 2003 from Stagecoach East London. It received a livery reminiscent of Stratford Blue, which it kept when the vehicle returned to Stagecoach ownership in February 2007 and was officially renumbered 12565. Derngate bus station in Northampton never witnessed Routemaster operation and today a theatre occupies the site. At this location on 2 March 2013 the bus awaits a wedding party from the nearby Guildhall. (Author's collection)

The Transport Museum Wythall, located to the south of Birmingham, has something on offer to please any era of interest. A wide range vehicles belonging to operators in the West Midlands are to be found, with the example shown a true 'Brummie'! 6835 was the last of five pre-production MCW Metrobuses new to West Midlands PTE in 1978 and built locally at Washwood Heath. It was exhibited at the 1978 Motor Show, held at the NEC, and served the public of Birmingham for nearly two decades before retiring in May 1998. Still looking clean and stylish, the bus was resting in one of the museum's on-site buildings on 8 October 2015.

The sights, sounds and smells of the past can certainly be appreciated at the Black Country Living Museum in Dudley along with the opportunity to view or even travel on vehicles now confined to history books. A trolley bus route exists within the grounds with a number of such vehicles in use. Waiting outside the 'depot' on 5 January 2010 was 433 (DUK 833), a Wolverhampton-built Sunbeam W4 with bodywork by Roe new in 1946 to Wolverhampton Corporation, operating until 1967. During our journey we have seen the reintroduction of trams but this mode of transport has yet to make a comeback.